50 Desserts to Impress

By: Kelly Johnson

Table of Contents

- Tiramisu
- Crème Brûlée
- Pavlova
- Chocolate Lava Cake
- Mille-feuille
- Eclairs
- Profiteroles
- Raspberry Macarons
- Lemon Meringue Pie
- Churros with Chocolate Sauce
- Baked Alaska
- Flourless Chocolate Cake
- Panna Cotta
- Baklava
- Opera Cake
- Cheesecake
- Key Lime Pie
- Black Forest Cake
- Charlotte Russe
- Sachertorte
- Sticky Toffee Pudding
- Soufflé
- Banoffee Pie
- Gateau St. Honoré
- Tarte Tatin
- Angel Food Cake
- Mochi Ice Cream
- Berry Trifle
- Carrot Cake
- Chocolate Fondant
- Tres Leches Cake
- Croquembouche
- Peach Melba
- Matcha Roll Cake
- Almond Tart

- Zabaione
- Fudge Brownies
- Chiffon Cake
- Semifreddo
- Coconut Cream Pie
- Fruit Tart
- Pumpkin Roll
- Pineapple Upside-Down Cake
- Chocolate Mousse
- Strawberry Shortcake
- Rice Pudding
- Poached Pears
- Cannoli
- Apricot Galette
- Lemon Ricotta Cake

Classic Italian Tiramisu

Ingredients:

- 6 large egg yolks
- 3/4 cup granulated sugar
- 1 cup mascarpone cheese
- 1 1/2 cups heavy cream
- 2 cups strong brewed coffee, cooled
- 1/4 cup coffee liqueur (optional)
- 2 packages (7 oz each) of ladyfingers
- Unsweetened cocoa powder, for dusting
- Dark chocolate shavings (optional)

Instructions:

1. In a large mixing bowl, whisk the egg yolks and sugar together until thick and pale.
2. Add the mascarpone cheese to the egg yolk mixture and beat until smooth.
3. In a separate bowl, whip the heavy cream until stiff peaks form. Gently fold the whipped cream into the mascarpone mixture.
4. Combine the coffee and coffee liqueur (if using) in a shallow dish.
5. Quickly dip each ladyfinger into the coffee mixture, ensuring they are moistened but not soggy.
6. Arrange a layer of dipped ladyfingers in the bottom of a 9x13 inch dish.
7. Spread half of the mascarpone mixture over the ladyfingers.
8. Add another layer of dipped ladyfingers, followed by the remaining mascarpone mixture.
9. Smooth the top and dust with unsweetened cocoa powder. Add chocolate shavings if desired.
10. Cover and refrigerate for at least 4 hours, preferably overnight, to allow the flavors to meld together.

Crème Brûlée

Ingredients:

- 4 cups heavy cream
- 1 vanilla bean, split and scraped
- 8 large egg yolks
- 1/2 cup granulated sugar
- 1/2 cup brown sugar (for topping)

Instructions:

1. Preheat oven to 325°F (160°C).
2. Heat the cream and vanilla bean in a saucepan over medium heat until hot but not boiling. Remove from heat and let cool slightly.
3. In a bowl, whisk together egg yolks and granulated sugar until pale and thick.
4. Slowly pour the hot cream into the egg mixture, whisking constantly.
5. Strain the mixture and pour into ramekins.
6. Place ramekins in a baking dish and fill the dish with hot water halfway up the sides of the ramekins.
7. Bake for 40-45 minutes until set but still slightly jiggly in the center.
8. Cool to room temperature, then refrigerate for at least 2 hours.
9. Before serving, sprinkle brown sugar on top and caramelize with a kitchen torch.

Pavlova

Ingredients:

- 4 large egg whites
- 1 cup granulated sugar
- 1 teaspoon white vinegar
- 1 teaspoon cornstarch
- 1 teaspoon vanilla extract
- Fresh berries and whipped cream for topping

Instructions:

1. Preheat oven to 250°F (120°C). Line a baking sheet with parchment paper.
2. Beat egg whites until soft peaks form.
3. Gradually add sugar, beating until stiff peaks form and the sugar is dissolved.
4. Gently fold in vinegar, cornstarch, and vanilla extract.
5. Spoon the meringue onto the baking sheet, shaping into a circle with slightly raised edges.
6. Bake for 1 hour, then turn off the oven and let the pavlova cool inside with the door slightly ajar.
7. Once cool, top with whipped cream and fresh berries.

Chocolate Lava Cake

Ingredients:

- 1/2 cup unsalted butter
- 6 ounces semi-sweet chocolate
- 2 large eggs
- 2 large egg yolks
- 1/4 cup granulated sugar
- 1/4 teaspoon salt
- 2 tablespoons all-purpose flour

Instructions:

1. Preheat oven to 450°F (230°C). Grease ramekins.
2. Melt butter and chocolate in a double boiler or microwave until smooth.
3. In a bowl, beat eggs, egg yolks, sugar, and salt until thickened.
4. Slowly add the chocolate mixture to the egg mixture, then fold in flour.
5. Divide batter among ramekins and bake for 10-12 minutes.
6. Let cool slightly, then invert onto plates and serve.

Mille-feuille

Ingredients:

- 1 package puff pastry
- 2 cups pastry cream
- 1/2 cup powdered sugar
- 1/4 cup dark chocolate, melted

Instructions:

1. Preheat oven to 400°F (200°C). Roll out puff pastry and cut into rectangles.
2. Bake on a parchment-lined sheet until golden brown. Let cool.
3. Layer pastry rectangles with pastry cream in between.
4. Top with powdered sugar or a drizzle of melted chocolate.

Eclairs

Ingredients:

- 1/2 cup water
- 1/2 cup milk
- 1/2 cup unsalted butter
- 1 cup all-purpose flour
- 4 large eggs
- Pastry cream for filling
- Chocolate glaze for topping

Instructions:

1. Preheat oven to 400°F (200°C). Line a baking sheet with parchment paper.
2. Heat water, milk, and butter in a saucepan until boiling.
3. Add flour and stir until a dough forms.
4. Remove from heat and let cool slightly. Beat in eggs one at a time.
5. Pipe dough onto the baking sheet and bake for 20-25 minutes.
6. Let cool, then fill with pastry cream and top with chocolate glaze.

Profiteroles

Ingredients:

- Same as eclairs

Instructions:

1. Follow the eclair dough recipe but pipe small rounds.
2. Bake for 20-25 minutes, cool, then fill with whipped cream or ice cream.
3. Top with chocolate sauce.

Raspberry Macarons

Ingredients:

- 1 cup powdered sugar
- 3/4 cup almond flour
- 2 large egg whites
- 1/4 cup granulated sugar
- Red food coloring
- Raspberry jam for filling

Instructions:

1. Preheat oven to 300°F (150°C). Line a baking sheet with parchment paper.
2. Sift powdered sugar and almond flour.
3. Beat egg whites until foamy, then add granulated sugar until stiff peaks form.
4. Fold in dry ingredients and food coloring.
5. Pipe small rounds onto the sheet and let sit for 30 minutes.
6. Bake for 15-18 minutes. Let cool, then fill with raspberry jam.

Lemon Meringue Pie

Ingredients:

- 1 pre-baked pie crust
- 1 cup granulated sugar
- 1/4 cup cornstarch
- 1 1/2 cups water
- 3 large egg yolks
- 1/4 cup lemon juice
- 1 tablespoon lemon zest
- 2 tablespoons butter
- 3 large egg whites
- 1/4 cup sugar (for meringue)

Instructions:

1. In a saucepan, whisk sugar, cornstarch, and water. Cook until thickened.
2. Add egg yolks, lemon juice, and zest, and cook until smooth.
3. Stir in butter and pour into the crust.
4. Beat egg whites until soft peaks form, then add sugar and beat until stiff peaks.
5. Spread meringue over the pie and bake at 350°F (175°C) for 10-12 minutes.

Churros with Chocolate Sauce

Ingredients:

- 1 cup water
- 2 1/2 tablespoons sugar
- 1/2 teaspoon salt
- 2 tablespoons vegetable oil
- 1 cup all-purpose flour
- Oil for frying
- 1/2 cup sugar mixed with 1 teaspoon cinnamon (for coating)
- 1/2 cup heavy cream
- 4 ounces dark chocolate

Instructions:

1. Boil water, sugar, salt, and oil in a saucepan.
2. Remove from heat and stir in flour.
3. Pipe dough into hot oil and fry until golden.
4. Roll in cinnamon sugar.
5. For the sauce, heat cream and pour over chocolate. Stir until smooth.

Baked Alaska

Ingredients:

- 1 quart vanilla ice cream
- 1 sponge cake layer (about 9 inches)
- 6 large egg whites
- 1/2 cup granulated sugar

Instructions:

1. Preheat the oven to 500°F (260°C).
2. Place the sponge cake on a baking sheet.
3. Spread the ice cream over the cake, forming a dome. Freeze until firm.
4. Beat egg whites until soft peaks form, then gradually add sugar and beat until stiff peaks form.
5. Cover the ice cream and cake with meringue, making sure it is sealed.
6. Bake for 3-5 minutes until the meringue is golden. Serve immediately.

Flourless Chocolate Cake

Ingredients:

- 8 ounces dark chocolate, chopped
- 1/2 cup unsalted butter
- 3/4 cup granulated sugar
- 1/4 teaspoon salt
- 4 large eggs
- 1/2 cup cocoa powder

Instructions:

1. Preheat oven to 375°F (190°C). Grease an 8-inch round pan.
2. Melt chocolate and butter together.
3. Stir in sugar and salt, then beat in eggs one at a time.
4. Add cocoa powder and mix until smooth.
5. Pour batter into the pan and bake for 25 minutes.
6. Let cool before serving.

Panna Cotta

Ingredients:

- 1 cup whole milk
- 1 tablespoon unflavored gelatin
- 2 cups heavy cream
- 1/2 cup sugar
- 1 teaspoon vanilla extract

Instructions:

1. Sprinkle gelatin over milk and let stand for 5 minutes.
2. Heat cream and sugar until dissolved, then add gelatin mixture.
3. Stir in vanilla and pour into molds.
4. Refrigerate for at least 4 hours before serving.

Baklava

Ingredients:

- 1 pound phyllo dough
- 1 cup unsalted butter, melted
- 1 pound chopped nuts
- 1 teaspoon ground cinnamon
- 1 cup granulated sugar
- 1 cup water
- 1/2 cup honey
- 1 teaspoon vanilla extract
- 1 teaspoon grated lemon zest

Instructions:

1. Preheat oven to 350°F (175°C). Butter a 9x13 inch pan.
2. Layer phyllo sheets in the pan, brushing each with butter, until half the sheets are used.
3. Mix nuts and cinnamon and sprinkle over the phyllo.
4. Layer remaining phyllo sheets, buttering each.
5. Cut into squares and bake for 50 minutes.
6. Boil sugar, water, honey, vanilla, and lemon zest for 10 minutes. Pour over baklava and let cool.

Opera Cake

Ingredients:

- Joconde sponge cake
- Coffee syrup
- Coffee buttercream
- Chocolate ganache
- Chocolate glaze

Instructions:

1. Layer the sponge cake with coffee syrup, buttercream, and ganache.
2. Repeat the layers, finishing with ganache.
3. Refrigerate until firm, then pour glaze over the top.
4. Chill before slicing.

Cheesecake

Ingredients:

- 1 1/2 cups graham cracker crumbs
- 1/4 cup melted butter
- 3 (8 ounce) packages cream cheese
- 1 cup sugar
- 1 teaspoon vanilla extract
- 3 large eggs

Instructions:

1. Preheat oven to 325°F (160°C).
2. Mix crumbs and butter, press into a springform pan.
3. Beat cream cheese, sugar, and vanilla until smooth.
4. Add eggs one at a time, beating after each addition.
5. Pour over the crust and bake for 50 minutes.
6. Cool before serving.

Key Lime Pie

Ingredients:

- 1 1/2 cups graham cracker crumbs
- 1/4 cup sugar
- 1/2 cup melted butter
- 3 large egg yolks
- 1 can sweetened condensed milk
- 1/2 cup key lime juice
- Whipped cream for topping

Instructions:

1. Preheat oven to 350°F (175°C).
2. Mix crumbs, sugar, and butter, then press into a pie dish.
3. Bake for 10 minutes, then cool.
4. Beat yolks and condensed milk, then stir in lime juice.
5. Pour filling into the crust and bake for 15 minutes.
6. Cool and refrigerate before serving.

Black Forest Cake

Ingredients:

- 1 chocolate cake, split into 3 layers
- 1/2 cup cherry liqueur
- 1 cup cherry pie filling
- 2 cups whipped cream
- Chocolate shavings

Instructions:

1. Sprinkle cake layers with cherry liqueur.
2. Spread cherry filling over the first layer, then add whipped cream.
3. Repeat with the second layer.
4. Place the final layer and cover the entire cake with whipped cream.
5. Garnish with chocolate shavings.

Charlotte Russe

Ingredients:

- Ladyfingers
- 2 cups heavy cream
- 1/2 cup sugar
- 1 teaspoon vanilla extract
- 1 envelope gelatin
- Fresh fruit for decoration

Instructions:

1. Line a mold with ladyfingers.
2. Whip cream with sugar and vanilla until stiff.
3. Dissolve gelatin in water and fold into the cream.
4. Fill the mold with the mixture and chill until set.
5. Unmold and decorate with fruit.

Sachertorte

Ingredients:

- 1/2 cup unsalted butter
- 4 ounces dark chocolate
- 1/2 cup granulated sugar
- 4 large eggs, separated
- 1/2 cup all-purpose flour
- 1/4 cup apricot jam
- 1/2 cup heavy cream
- 4 ounces dark chocolate (for glaze)

Instructions:

1. Preheat oven to 350°F (175°C). Grease a 9-inch round pan.
2. Melt butter and chocolate. Stir in sugar and egg yolks.
3. Beat egg whites to stiff peaks and fold into chocolate mixture.
4. Fold in flour and pour into the pan.
5. Bake for 30 minutes and cool.
6. Spread jam over the cake.
7. Heat cream and pour over chocolate to make glaze. Pour over cake.

Sticky Toffee Pudding

Ingredients:

- 1 cup chopped dates
- 1 cup boiling water
- 1 teaspoon baking soda
- 1/4 cup butter
- 3/4 cup brown sugar
- 2 large eggs
- 1 cup all-purpose flour
- 1 teaspoon baking powder

Instructions:

1. Preheat oven to 350°F (175°C).
2. Soak dates in boiling water with baking soda.
3. Cream butter and sugar, beat in eggs, then fold in flour and baking powder.
4. Stir in date mixture and pour into a greased pan.
5. Bake for 35 minutes. Serve with toffee sauce.

Soufflé

Ingredients:

- 2 tablespoons butter
- 2 tablespoons flour
- 1 cup milk
- 4 large eggs, separated
- 1/2 cup grated cheese (for savory) or sugar (for sweet)

Instructions:

1. Preheat oven to 375°F (190°C). Butter a soufflé dish.
2. Make a roux with butter and flour, whisk in milk until thickened.
3. Remove from heat, beat in egg yolks and cheese/sugar.
4. Beat egg whites to stiff peaks and fold into the mixture.
5. Pour into the dish and bake for 25 minutes.

Banoffee Pie

Ingredients:

- 1 1/2 cups graham cracker crumbs
- 1/2 cup butter, melted
- 1 can sweetened condensed milk (caramelized)
- 3 bananas, sliced
- 2 cups whipped cream
- Chocolate shavings for garnish

Instructions:

1. Mix crumbs and butter, press into a pie dish.
2. Spread caramel over the crust, then layer with bananas.
3. Top with whipped cream and garnish with chocolate.

Gateau St. Honoré

Ingredients:

- Puff pastry
- Choux pastry (for profiteroles)
- 1 cup sugar
- 2 cups heavy cream
- 1/2 cup sugar (for cream)
- 1 teaspoon vanilla extract

Instructions:

1. Bake puff pastry and profiteroles.
2. Make caramel with sugar and water.
3. Fill profiteroles with whipped cream and dip in caramel.
4. Arrange on puff pastry and fill the center with whipped cream.

Tarte Tatin

Ingredients:

- 6 apples, peeled and sliced
- 1/2 cup butter
- 3/4 cup sugar
- 1 sheet puff pastry

Instructions:

1. Preheat oven to 375°F (190°C).
2. Melt butter and sugar in a skillet, add apples and cook until caramelized.
3. Cover with puff pastry and bake for 30 minutes.
4. Invert onto a plate to serve.

Angel Food Cake

Ingredients:

- 1 cup cake flour
- 1 1/2 cups sugar
- 12 large egg whites
- 1 teaspoon cream of tartar
- 1 teaspoon vanilla extract

Instructions:

1. Preheat oven to 350°F (175°C).
2. Sift flour and half the sugar.
3. Beat egg whites, cream of tartar, and vanilla to soft peaks, then add sugar.
4. Fold in flour mixture and pour into an ungreased tube pan.
5. Bake for 35 minutes and cool upside down.

Mochi Ice Cream

Ingredients:

- 1 cup glutinous rice flour
- 1/4 cup sugar
- 3/4 cup water
- Ice cream (any flavor)

Instructions:

1. Mix flour, sugar, and water, then microwave for 2 minutes, stirring halfway.
2. Dust a surface with cornstarch and roll out the dough.
3. Cut into circles, place a scoop of ice cream, and wrap.
4. Freeze until firm.

Berry Trifle

Ingredients:

- 1 pound cake
- 2 cups mixed berries
- 2 cups custard
- 2 cups whipped cream

Instructions:

1. Layer slices of pound cake in a trifle dish.
2. Add a layer of berries, followed by custard and whipped cream.
3. Repeat layers, finishing with whipped cream and berries on top.
4. Chill before serving.

Carrot Cake

Ingredients:

- 2 cups all-purpose flour
- 2 teaspoons baking powder
- 1 1/2 teaspoons baking soda
- 2 teaspoons ground cinnamon
- 1/2 teaspoon ground nutmeg
- 1/2 teaspoon salt
- 1 1/2 cups vegetable oil
- 1 1/2 cups granulated sugar
- 1/2 cup brown sugar
- 4 large eggs
- 2 teaspoons vanilla extract
- 3 cups grated carrots
- 1 cup chopped walnuts (optional)
- 1/2 cup raisins (optional)

Instructions:

1. Preheat oven to 350°F (175°C). Grease two 9-inch round cake pans.
2. In a bowl, combine flour, baking powder, baking soda, cinnamon, nutmeg, and salt.
3. In another bowl, mix oil, sugars, eggs, and vanilla until smooth.
4. Gradually add the dry ingredients, then fold in carrots, walnuts, and raisins.
5. Divide the batter between the pans and bake for 35-40 minutes. Cool before frosting.

Chocolate Fondant

Ingredients:

- 1/2 cup unsalted butter
- 4 ounces dark chocolate
- 2 large eggs
- 2 large egg yolks
- 1/4 cup granulated sugar
- 2 tablespoons all-purpose flour

Instructions:

1. Preheat oven to 425°F (220°C). Butter and flour ramekins.
2. Melt butter and chocolate together. Beat eggs, yolks, and sugar until thick.
3. Fold chocolate into the egg mixture, then gently fold in flour.
4. Pour into ramekins and bake for 12 minutes. Serve warm.

Tres Leches Cake

Ingredients:

- 1 cup all-purpose flour
- 1 1/2 teaspoons baking powder
- 1/4 teaspoon salt
- 5 large eggs, separated
- 1 cup granulated sugar
- 1/3 cup whole milk
- 1 teaspoon vanilla extract
- 1 can evaporated milk
- 1 can sweetened condensed milk
- 1/3 cup heavy cream

Instructions:

1. Preheat oven to 350°F (175°C). Grease a 9x13 inch pan.
2. Sift flour, baking powder, and salt. Beat egg yolks and sugar until light.
3. Add milk and vanilla, then fold in the flour mixture.
4. Beat egg whites to stiff peaks and fold into the batter.
5. Pour into the pan and bake for 25-30 minutes.
6. Combine the three milks and pour over the cooled cake. Chill before serving.

Croquembouche

Ingredients:

- 1 cup water
- 1/2 cup butter
- 1 cup all-purpose flour
- 4 large eggs
- 1 cup sugar (for caramel)

Instructions:

1. Preheat oven to 425°F (220°C). Line a baking sheet with parchment paper.
2. Boil water and butter, add flour, and stir until a dough forms.
3. Add eggs one at a time, mixing well.
4. Pipe dough into small mounds and bake for 20 minutes.
5. Melt sugar to make caramel. Dip each puff in caramel and stack into a cone shape.

Peach Melba

Ingredients:

- 4 ripe peaches
- 1/2 cup sugar
- 1 vanilla bean
- 1 pint raspberry sauce
- Vanilla ice cream

Instructions:

1. Boil peaches in water until skins loosen, then peel and slice.
2. Heat sugar and vanilla with water to make a syrup.
3. Poach peaches in the syrup for 10 minutes.
4. Serve with raspberry sauce and vanilla ice cream.

Matcha Roll Cake

Ingredients:

- 3 large eggs
- 1/2 cup sugar
- 3/4 cup cake flour
- 1 tablespoon matcha powder
- 1/2 cup heavy cream
- 2 tablespoons powdered sugar

Instructions:

1. Preheat oven to 350°F (175°C). Line a baking sheet with parchment paper.
2. Beat eggs and sugar until thick. Sift flour and matcha, fold into the egg mixture.
3. Pour into the baking sheet and bake for 10-12 minutes.
4. Beat heavy cream and powdered sugar to stiff peaks.
5. Spread cream on the cooled cake, roll it up, and chill before slicing.

Almond Tart

Ingredients:

- 1 1/4 cups all-purpose flour
- 1/4 cup sugar
- 1/2 cup unsalted butter, cold
- 1 large egg yolk
- 2 tablespoons water
- 1/2 cup almond paste
- 1/2 cup sugar
- 2 large eggs
- 1/4 cup all-purpose flour
- 1/4 cup unsalted butter, melted

Instructions:

1. Preheat oven to 375°F (190°C). Grease a tart pan.
2. Mix flour and sugar, cut in butter until crumbly. Add egg yolk and water to form dough.
3. Roll out and press into the tart pan.
4. Beat almond paste, sugar, and eggs until smooth. Add flour and melted butter.
5. Pour into the crust and bake for 35 minutes.

Zabaione

Ingredients:

- 4 large egg yolks
- 1/4 cup sugar
- 1/2 cup Marsala wine

Instructions:

1. Beat egg yolks and sugar in a bowl over simmering water.
2. Gradually add Marsala, whisking until thickened.
3. Serve warm or chilled.

Fudge Brownies

Ingredients:

- 1/2 cup unsalted butter
- 1 cup sugar
- 2 large eggs
- 1 teaspoon vanilla extract
- 1/3 cup unsweetened cocoa powder
- 1/2 cup all-purpose flour
- 1/4 teaspoon salt
- 1/4 teaspoon baking powder

Instructions:

1. Preheat oven to 350°F (175°C). Grease a 9x9 inch pan.
2. Melt butter, stir in sugar, eggs, and vanilla.
3. Add cocoa, flour, salt, and baking powder. Mix well.
4. Pour into the pan and bake for 20-25 minutes.

Chiffon Cake

Ingredients:

- 2 1/4 cups cake flour
- 1 1/2 cups granulated sugar
- 1 tablespoon baking powder
- 1/2 teaspoon salt
- 1/2 cup vegetable oil
- 7 large egg yolks
- 3/4 cup water
- 1 tablespoon vanilla extract
- 7 large egg whites
- 1/2 teaspoon cream of tartar

Instructions:

1. Preheat oven to 325°F (165°C). Do not grease the pan.
2. Sift flour, sugar, baking powder, and salt into a bowl.
3. In another bowl, beat oil, egg yolks, water, and vanilla.
4. Combine wet and dry ingredients until smooth.
5. Beat egg whites and cream of tartar until stiff peaks form.
6. Fold egg whites into the batter gently.
7. Pour into a tube pan and bake for 55-60 minutes.
8. Invert the pan to cool completely before removing the cake.

Semifreddo

Ingredients:

- 4 large eggs
- 1/2 cup sugar
- 2 cups heavy cream
- 1 teaspoon vanilla extract

Instructions:

1. Whisk eggs and sugar over a simmering water bath until thickened.
2. Remove from heat and continue whisking until cool.
3. In another bowl, whip cream and vanilla to soft peaks.
4. Fold whipped cream into the egg mixture.
5. Pour into a loaf pan, cover, and freeze for at least 4 hours.

Coconut Cream Pie

Ingredients:

- 1 9-inch pie crust, pre-baked
- 1/2 cup sugar
- 1/4 cup cornstarch
- 1/4 teaspoon salt
- 2 cups whole milk
- 1 cup coconut milk
- 3 large egg yolks
- 1/2 cup shredded coconut
- 1 teaspoon vanilla extract
- Whipped cream and toasted coconut for topping

Instructions:

1. In a saucepan, whisk sugar, cornstarch, and salt. Gradually add milk and coconut milk.
2. Cook over medium heat until thick, then stir in egg yolks and continue cooking for 2 minutes.
3. Remove from heat, add shredded coconut and vanilla.
4. Pour into the crust, cool, and chill for 4 hours.
5. Top with whipped cream and toasted coconut before serving.

Fruit Tart

Ingredients:

- 1 1/4 cups all-purpose flour
- 1/4 cup sugar
- 1/2 cup unsalted butter, cold
- 1 large egg yolk
- 2 tablespoons water
- 1 cup pastry cream
- Assorted fresh fruits

Instructions:

1. Preheat oven to 375°F (190°C). Grease a tart pan.
2. Mix flour and sugar, cut in butter until crumbly. Add egg yolk and water to form dough.
3. Roll out and press into the tart pan. Bake for 20-25 minutes.
4. Cool, fill with pastry cream, and top with fresh fruits.

Pumpkin Roll

Ingredients:

- 3/4 cup all-purpose flour
- 1/2 teaspoon baking powder
- 1/2 teaspoon baking soda
- 1/2 teaspoon ground cinnamon
- 1/2 teaspoon ground ginger
- 1/4 teaspoon ground nutmeg
- 1/4 teaspoon salt
- 3 large eggs
- 1 cup granulated sugar
- 2/3 cup pumpkin puree
- 1 cup cream cheese, softened
- 1 cup powdered sugar
- 6 tablespoons butter, softened
- 1 teaspoon vanilla extract

Instructions:

1. Preheat oven to 375°F (190°C). Line a jelly roll pan with parchment paper.
2. Sift flour, baking powder, soda, spices, and salt.
3. Beat eggs and sugar until thick. Add pumpkin and mix.
4. Fold in the dry ingredients, spread in the pan, and bake for 13-15 minutes.
5. Cool, spread with cream cheese filling, and roll tightly.

Pineapple Upside-Down Cake

Ingredients:

- 1/4 cup unsalted butter
- 1/2 cup brown sugar
- 1 can pineapple rings
- Maraschino cherries
- 1 1/2 cups all-purpose flour
- 1 teaspoon baking powder
- 1/2 teaspoon baking soda
- 1/4 teaspoon salt
- 1/2 cup unsalted butter, softened
- 1 cup granulated sugar
- 2 large eggs
- 1 teaspoon vanilla extract
- 3/4 cup buttermilk

Instructions:

1. Preheat oven to 350°F (175°C). Melt butter in a skillet, add brown sugar, and arrange pineapple rings and cherries.
2. Mix flour, baking powder, soda, and salt.
3. Cream butter and sugar, add eggs and vanilla. Mix in dry ingredients alternately with buttermilk.
4. Pour batter over pineapples and bake for 35-40 minutes.
5. Cool for 5 minutes, then invert onto a plate.

Chocolate Mousse

Ingredients:

- 4 ounces dark chocolate
- 2 tablespoons unsalted butter
- 2 large eggs, separated
- 1/4 cup sugar
- 1/2 cup heavy cream
- 1 teaspoon vanilla extract

Instructions:

1. Melt chocolate and butter. Beat egg yolks with sugar until thick.
2. Stir yolks into the chocolate mixture.
3. Whip cream and vanilla to soft peaks, fold into chocolate.
4. Beat egg whites to stiff peaks and gently fold in.
5. Chill for at least 2 hours before serving.

Strawberry Shortcake

Ingredients:

- 2 cups all-purpose flour
- 1/4 cup sugar
- 1 tablespoon baking powder
- 1/2 teaspoon salt
- 1/2 cup unsalted butter, cold
- 2/3 cup milk
- 2 cups sliced strawberries
- 1/4 cup sugar
- Whipped cream

Instructions:

1. Preheat oven to 425°F (220°C). Mix flour, sugar, baking powder, and salt.
2. Cut in butter until crumbly. Add milk and stir to form dough.
3. Roll out, cut into rounds, and bake for 12-15 minutes.
4. Toss strawberries with sugar. Slice shortcakes and fill with strawberries and whipped cream.

Rice Pudding

Ingredients:

- 1/2 cup uncooked white rice
- 4 cups whole milk
- 1/2 cup sugar
- 1/4 teaspoon salt
- 1/2 teaspoon vanilla extract
- 1/2 teaspoon ground cinnamon (optional)
- 1/4 cup raisins (optional)

Instructions:

1. In a saucepan, combine rice, milk, sugar, and salt. Cook over medium heat, stirring occasionally, until the mixture thickens, about 30-40 minutes.
2. Remove from heat and stir in vanilla extract. Add cinnamon and raisins if desired.
3. Serve warm or chilled.

Poached Pears

Ingredients:

- 4 ripe pears, peeled and cored
- 4 cups water
- 1 cup sugar
- 1 vanilla bean, split (or 1 teaspoon vanilla extract)
- 1 cinnamon stick (optional)
- Zest of 1 lemon (optional)

Instructions:

1. In a large saucepan, bring water, sugar, vanilla bean, cinnamon stick, and lemon zest to a simmer.
2. Add pears and simmer gently for 25-30 minutes until tender.
3. Remove pears and let cool. Serve with the poaching liquid as a syrup.

Cannoli

Ingredients:

- 2 cups ricotta cheese
- 1/2 cup powdered sugar
- 1/2 teaspoon vanilla extract
- 1/4 cup mini chocolate chips
- 12 cannoli shells

Instructions:

1. In a bowl, mix ricotta cheese, powdered sugar, and vanilla until smooth.
2. Fold in chocolate chips.
3. Fill cannoli shells with the ricotta mixture.
4. Dust with powdered sugar before serving.

Apricot Galette

Ingredients:

- 1 pre-made pie crust
- 5-6 apricots, sliced
- 1/4 cup sugar
- 1 tablespoon cornstarch
- 1 teaspoon lemon juice
- 1 tablespoon unsalted butter, melted

Instructions:

1. Preheat oven to 375°F (190°C). Roll out pie crust on a baking sheet.
2. Toss apricots with sugar, cornstarch, and lemon juice.
3. Arrange apricots in the center of the crust, leaving a 2-inch border.
4. Fold edges of the crust over the fruit, brush with melted butter.
5. Bake for 35-40 minutes until golden.

Lemon Ricotta Cake

Ingredients:

- 1 1/2 cups all-purpose flour
- 2 teaspoons baking powder
- 1/2 teaspoon salt
- 3/4 cup sugar
- 1/2 cup unsalted butter, softened
- 3 large eggs
- 1 cup ricotta cheese
- Zest and juice of 1 lemon
- 1 teaspoon vanilla extract

Instructions:

1. Preheat oven to 350°F (175°C). Grease a 9-inch cake pan.
2. Mix flour, baking powder, and salt in a bowl.
3. In another bowl, beat sugar and butter until fluffy. Add eggs one at a time.
4. Mix in ricotta, lemon zest, juice, and vanilla.
5. Gradually add dry ingredients, mixing until just combined.
6. Pour batter into the pan and bake for 35-40 minutes.
7. Cool before serving, optionally dust with powdered sugar.